KW-756-470

All the Flavours in the World

Pamela Rushby

Illustrated by
Craig Smith

GINN

GINN

This book is copyright and reproduction of the whole or part
without the publishers' written permission is prohibited.
© Heinemann Australia 1992

1996 UK edition published by Ginn and Company Limited
Prebendal House, Parson's Fee, Aylesbury, Bucks HP20 2QY
ISBN 0 602 27010 3

Printed in Hong Kong by Dah Hua Printing Press Co., Ltd.

Reprinted in 1997

Contents

Chapter One

Books, bags and basketball boots

Can you think of anything more boring than back-to-school shopping? If you can, you deserve a prize.

There you are, the holidays nearly over, and your mother wants to waste your time shopping for exercise books. And clear, sticky stuff to cover them with. And lunchboxes. And schoolbags. And shoes.

And it's no good saying, "You choose the bag, Mum. I'll be happy with whatever you pick. I'll just go swimming instead." Because your mother will only say, "But Pete, you have to be there to try the shoes on, dear. And while we're out we may as well pick up those exercise books and a new lunchbox and..."

Swimming? Forget it. You're going shopping. You might as well write off the whole day.

So there we were in the mall, Mum and my little sister, Jenna, and me. Outside it was hot and sunny and my friends were all at the pool.

Inside, the mall was full of people with worried-looking faces, and bright, glaring lights and really daggy piped music.

The one good thing about the mall is the ice cream shop. It has heaps of flavours. I've never counted them all, but there must be about forty. Mum usually buys Jenna and me an ice cream when we've finished the shopping. But today I wasn't sure. Mum was frowning as she added up all the money she'd had to spend. Somehow, I didn't think we were going to get ice cream.

Mum had already bought two big new schoolbags and a pile of exercise books. I had a new pair of school shoes—heavy black leather that felt like lumps of concrete around my feet.

Now it was Jenna's turn. The shop assistant carried out a pile of boxes. I knew this was going to take a long time. Jenna has what Mum calls "hard-to-fit" feet.

"Mum?" I said hopefully. "Could I go and get an ice cream while Jenna's trying on shoes?"

Jenna gave me a dirty look. Mum didn't hear me. She was watching the assistant feel for Jenna's toes in the shoes they'd just put on her.

"Mum?" I said. "Not now, dear," said Mum. "I'm busy."

I sighed. I looked around the shop. Bo-o-o-o-ring. Then, at the back of the shop, I saw something interesting. Doc Martens. Wow! I thought. I tried one on. It was big and black and clumpy. Like my new school shoes. The difference was, these were totally cool.

"Mum?" I said, waving the Doc Martens at her. "Look! Unreal! Could I have these for school?"

The assistant gave me a sour look. He thought he'd finished with me. "The ones you've got are the right sort for your school," he said.

"But—" I said.

"Not NOW, Pete!" said Mum.

I put the Doc Martens back. Beside them I found a display of basketball boots. The very latest style. I tried a pair on. They felt great. I stood up and jumped gently up and down, trying them out.

The shop seemed to melt away, and a cheering crowd took its place. I was Powerhouse Pete, basketball legend. I could just see myself...

The last quarter. Ten seconds left on the clock. Powerhouse Pete steals the ball...he takes it down the court...watch this guy go...he goes straight through the other team...he jumps! He does the famous Powerhouse Pete double pump reverse backwards jam! He dunks it! It's magic! The crowd goes wild! Pete! Pete! Pete!

"Pete!" It wasn't a cheering crowd. It was Mum. She and the assistant were glaring at me. "Pete!" said Mum. "Take those boots off. Sit down and don't even think of moving again until I'm ready to go." She had that I've-had-about-enough look in her eye.

I put the boots back, sat down and stared out of the shop into the mall.

Outside I could see some kids I knew from school, Mike and Sally. They were shopping with their mother. It looked like the same back-to-school stuff. Sally had a shoe bag, and Mike a pile of books. They waved at me. I waved back. I liked Mike and Sally.

Then I saw someone else I knew from school. Someone I didn't want to see. Someone I didn't like at all. Slugger McShoo.

Chapter Two

Slugger

Slugger McShoo is the biggest and toughest kid in our school. And the meanest. Slugger didn't get his name from picking daisies.

Slugger's the sort of kid who takes little kids' lunch money off them. If they've brought their lunch, he flushes it down the toilet. He likes sneaking up and opening the catches on schoolbags so that all your stuff falls onto the ground. Then he stomps on it. It's best to keep right out of Slugger's way.

Sally and Mike's Mum had sat Sally down on a seat in the mall while she took Mike off to a shop nearby. Sally sat waiting. And Slugger sneaked up beside her, reaching out to snatch the shoe bag that Sally had left lying on the seat.

At least, he tried to. Because I stopped him. I waved wildly to Sally. She spun around, saw Slugger, and pulled her bag away. And two things happened.

The first was that Slugger saw me. He knew I'd warned Sally. He screwed his fist up and waved it in my direction. I knew what that meant. Prepare to die. Slugger was annoyed with me.

The second thing was that, as I waved my arms to warn Sally, I'd bumped into a display stand of shoes. Shoes crashed to the floor all around me. So Mum and the assistant were glaring at me again.

"Pete," said Mum. "Go and wait outside. Look, go and buy that ice cream you've been wanting. But just go outside. Just—go."

Five minutes ago I couldn't have got outside that shop fast enough. But now I didn't want to. Somewhere, out there, Slugger was waiting for me. If he caught up with me, I was dead meat. I tiptoed to the door and peered out. I couldn't see Slugger. Maybe if I was really careful...

I slid out the door. Uh oh! There was Slugger, just across the mall. He hadn't seen me yet. I glanced around. Beside me, down the side of the shoe shop, was a long corridor.

Funny, I'd never noticed that corridor before. At the end of it I could see lights flashing. I peered down. ICE CREAM! the lights flashed. ICE CREAM! ALL THE FLAVOURS IN THE WORLD!

Well, look at that, I thought. All the flavours in the world! This looked like the perfect place to keep away from Slugger. I slipped around the corner and bolted down the length of the corridor to the ice cream shop.

Chapter Three

Funny place for a shop

It really was strange, I thought, as I ran along the corridor. I'd never known this part of the mall existed. Funny place for an ice cream shop, too, right out of the way at the end of a long, dark corridor. I wasn't surprised to find I was the only customer.

There was a long, long counter with a glass top. Under the glass were hundreds and hundreds of ice cream containers, overflowing with ice cream, in all the colours you could imagine. ALL THE FLAVOURS IN THE WORLD! blinked the coloured lights. There was no-one there.

Then someone bobbed up from under the counter. She stopped when she saw me.

"A customer!" she said, with a big smile. And her smile was huge, because it was painted onto her face. She was wearing a kind of clown outfit, but hers was the prettiest one I'd ever seen. All pink and frilly, with a skirt that stuck right out and had layers and layers of frills under it, and little bells sewn all round the edges. Her hair was bright pink too, and wildly curly. You could say she wasn't your average shop assistant.

"What would you like?" asked the pink clown, smiling at me. "I have all the flavours in the world!"

I couldn't believe that. "ALL the flavours?" I said.

"Every one!"

"Are you sure?" I said.

The pink clown looked a bit surprised. "Absolutely!" she said. She pointed to the flashing lights. That's what it said, all right. All the flavours in the world.

OK, I thought. You asked for it. "Do you have—pink lemonade?" I asked.

"Of course!" The pink clown pointed to a container. Sure enough, the ice cream was bright pink. And the label read, PINK LEMONADE.

Lucky, I thought. Try again. "How about—
apple pie?"

"Without a doubt!" She pointed again. And
there it was. A container labelled, APPLE PIE.

I'll make one up! I thought. "Have you got,
um—hot buttered popcorn?"

The pink clown smiled. "Certainly!"

That ice cream looked a bit strange. It had
wisps of steam rising from it, and pieces of
popcorn sitting on top of the container. But
the label read, HOT BUTTERED POPCORN.

I was impressed. "You really have got every flavour in the world!" I said.

"Indeed I have," said the pink clown. "Anything you ask for! But—there is a rule."

"What's that?" I asked.

"You can have any flavour ice cream you ask for. Anything at all. But the rule is, once you ask for it, you must eat it. So choose carefully, please!"

"What happens if I don't eat it?" I asked.

The pink clown looked sad. "If you don't, then the ice cream shop will disappear. Completely. Forever. It'll never be here again."

I'd never seen it here before, but I didn't
want it to go away. There were a few flavours
I'd like to try. So I chose my ice cream
carefully. A double. Pink lemonade and hot
buttered popcorn. I offered my money to the
pink clown.

"Oh no," she said. "You don't pay at this
shop. The ice cream's free."

Free! I liked this shop! I didn't want it to
disappear. I hoped I'd like the flavours I'd
chosen. I wasn't absolutely sure about the hot
buttered popcorn. The pink clown watched
anxiously as I took a lick.

Delicious! I licked and licked. The pink clown relaxed.

There was a noise of running feet. Mike and Sally came rushing down the corridor. "Pete! Slugger's after us!" panted Sally. "And he's looking for you, too!"

Chapter Four

Spaghetti bolognaise

Slugger was after me! I can't say I wasn't scared. But I had other things to think about. "Look at this!" I said. "All the flavours in the world! And it's free!"

Mike and Sally stared at the containers of ice cream. "All the flavours in the world? Have you got—chocolate biscuit and cherry?" asked Sally.

"To be sure."

"Toasted marshmallow?" suggested Mike.

"By all means."

"Fairyfloss?"

"Unquestionably."

"Spaghetti bolognaise?"

Sally and I stared at Mike. "SPAGHETTI BOLOGNAISE??!!" we said.

"Why not?" said Mike. "I like spaghetti bolognaise!" He looked at the pink clown. "Have you got it?"

The pink clown nodded. "I have all the flavours in the world," she said proudly. "But—" she explained the rule to Sally and Mike. "So—please choose carefully," she finished.

Sally and Mike nodded. Sally chose fairyfloss. It was pink and sugary looking, with little wisps of spun sugar floating around it.

And Mike chose spaghetti bolognaise. It was a rich red colour. The pink clown plopped a scoop of it into the cone, then twisted the spaghetti up with a fork and balanced it on the top. She handed it to Mike.

Mike stared at it.

"You have to eat it," I said.

"I am, I am," said Mike. But he didn't lick it.

Did we imagine it, or did the lights on the ice cream shop flicker and dim a little? The pink clown glanced at them anxiously.

Slowly, Mike took a lick. He took another. He grinned. "Yum!" he said. The pink clown relaxed. The lights grew bright again. We all smiled at each other.

And Slugger came stomping along the corridor.

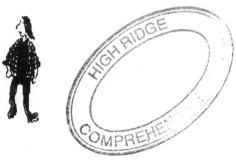

Chapter Five

Slugger's choice

Slugger stopped and glared at Mike, Sally and me. "You're dead meat," he said. He pointed at me. "You're first," he said. He started towards me, pushing up his sleeves.

"Wait!"said the pink clown. "Wouldn't you like an ice cream first?"

Slugger stopped. "A what?" he said.

"An ice cream," said the pink clown. "I have all the flavours in the world!"

"All the —" said Slugger. "You can't have! Nobody has all the flavours in the world."

"I do," said the pink clown.

"She does," Mike, Sally and I agreed.

Slugger stomped over and looked at the containers of ice cream. "Don't believe it!" he said.

"Try me," said the pink clown. "What flavour would you like?"

Slugger thought. It wasn't easy for him. You could just about hear his brain creaking. Then he grinned. It wasn't a pleasant grin.

"Have you got—mango and maggots?" he said.

The pink clown looked a little pale, but she nodded. "Undoubtedly."

Slugger frowned. He thought again. "Um, have you got—sweaty football socks and cheese?"

The pink clown swallowed. "Assuredly."

Slugger scowled. "What about—". His brain clicked and whirred. Inspiration struck. He grinned again. "What about cowpat and cream, furball and fleapowder, and mangrove mud with worm ripple?"

The pink clown put her chin up. "Naturally."

Slugger sneered. "I'll have that then," he said. "A triple."

"Is that your choice?" asked the pink clown.

Slugger grinned and nodded. We could see he thought he had her trapped.

"Very well,"said the pink clown. "But there is a rule—". She explained the rule to him.

"Sure, sure," sneered Slugger. "Anything you say. Just show me this ice cream. And don't forget the worm ripple."

The pink clown dipped her scoop into a container right at the back of the counter. Mike and Sally and I crowded around to look.

The ice cream looked—it looked—. Well, it looked just like cowpats. And furballs. And mangrove mud. And it was moving.

The ice cream was slowly heaving up and down, as worms crawled to the top, surfaced for a moment, then slid down to the bottom again.

"Are you sure about this?" said the pink clown to Slugger.

Slugger stretched his hand over the counter impatiently. The pink clown handed him the ice cream. Slugger took it.

Chapter Six

"Eat it!"

Slugger stared at the ice cream in his hand.
His eyes bulged. He couldn't believe it. The
worms crawled in, and the worms crawled out
again. The ice cream slowly oozed down his
fingers and dripped onto his sneakers. We all
watched him.

"You have to eat it," the pink clown said.

"Ye-e-ech!"said Slugger.

Did we imagine it, or did the lights on the ice cream shop flicker and seem to dim a little? The pink clown glanced at them anxiously. Sally and Mike and I looked at her. We turned to Slugger.

"You have to eat it," we said.

"Eat this muck? No way!" said Slugger.

This time we didn't imagine it. The lights were definitely growing dimmer. Sally and Mike and I looked at each other. We didn't want this incredible place to disappear. We turned back to Slugger.

"Eat it," I said.

Slugger glared at me. He couldn't believe I'd try to tell him what to do. Nobody had ever done that to him. "You're dead meat," he said. But somehow, it didn't sound as scary as it had before.

Sally and Mike and I closed in around him.

"Eat it," said Sally.

Suddenly Slugger was looking worried. We weren't scared of him any more. He didn't like it. He didn't know how to handle it. But he didn't lick the ice cream.

"YOU eat it," said Slugger.

The lights were growing dimmer. We didn't have much time. We moved in closer.

"Eat it," said Mike.

Slugger was really worried now. He knew we meant it. Even if we were smaller, we were three to one. Slugger knew he didn't stand a chance. But he didn't lick the ice cream.

"I d-d-don't want to," he said.

The lights were almost gone. We had to hurry. We closed in on Slugger, all around him, in a ring he couldn't escape.

"EAT IT," we said.

And Slugger did. He took a lick. He shuddered. He took another lick. And another. While we stood in a ring around him, he finished that ice cream. To the very last worm.

As he finished, the pink clown smiled. The lights grew bright again. And as they grew brighter, we could see Slugger's face was going a most interesting colour. Sort of pasty white, then turning greener and greener and greener.

The pink clown leaned helpfully over the counter. She pointed down the corridor. "The toilets are that way," she said.

Slugger clapped his hands over his mouth and raced off down the corridor. We watched him go.

"Do you think he'll make it?" said Sally.

Out in the mall, we could hear people shouting. "Look out!" "Stand aside!" "Let the kid through!" Then, "Oh, YUCK!"

"I don't think he made it," said the pink clown.

She leaned over the counter and tried to hug us all. "And I don't think he'll ever bother you again either," she said. "Now, what flavour would you like? I have—"

"All the flavours in the world!" we shouted together. We crowded around the counter to choose.

Chapter Seven

Slugger staggers off

When we walked out into the mall, licking our ice creams, Slugger was sitting drooping on a seat. He still looked green. A cleaner was working around him, with a mop and a bucket. She didn't look very happy with Slugger.

Slugger didn't look very happy when he saw our ice creams, either. He turned even greener, and he got up and staggered off without saying a word to us.

"I think the pink clown's right," I said to Mike and Sally. "Slugger'll never bother us again."

We looked back to wave goodbye to the pink clown. But the ice cream shop and the pink clown had gone. Vanished. Just like that.

You know, we've never found that ice cream shop again. Sally and Mike and I have searched all over the mall. There's no long, dark corridor beside the shoe shop. It's disappeared.

But one day, we hope, we'll be in the mall, maybe doing some really boring shopping, and an ice cream shop—an ice cream shop with a pink clown behind the counter—will just pop up out of nowhere.

Sort of like magic.